For permission requests, write to the publisher at the address below: Justwise Publications
PO BOX 1112
Mackay, QLD, 4740
Publishing@justwiseaccountingbooks.com

AF880017

DEDICATION

This book is dedicated to all book-loving readers. Your unwavering support and encouragement have been the cornerstone of this journey. Always remember—you can do it!

CONTENTS

FOREWORD

"Welcome to this book. It's a journey through timeless wisdom, quirky facts, and practical strategies for navigating the world of personal finance and investment. Whether you are intrigued by thought-provoking ideas, looking for engaging mental exercises, or analyzing incredible investment stories, such as turning $19k into $13 million, this book has something for you.

Each chapter is thoughtfully crafted to offer insights tailored to your interests—whether you are exploring economic concepts like inflation and deflation, expanding your thinking with big-picture perspectives, or diving into real-world examples of financial growth through disciplined investing.

This book invites you to reflect, grow, and take action. Whether you are a curious reader or a seasoned investor refining your strategies, you will find practical advice and inspiration for your personal and financial journey.

Thank you for choosing this book. May it spark new ideas, challenge your perspective, and empower you to think big and achieve even bigger."

CHAPTER 1 – "TIMELESS WISDOM"

" Keep Your Expenses Low & Guard Your Treasures from Loss " -
The Richest Man in Babylon [Book]

"A person trying to calculate expenses to guard his treasures"

" Invest for Retirement Secure your future with smart savings"-
The Richest Man in Babylon [Book]

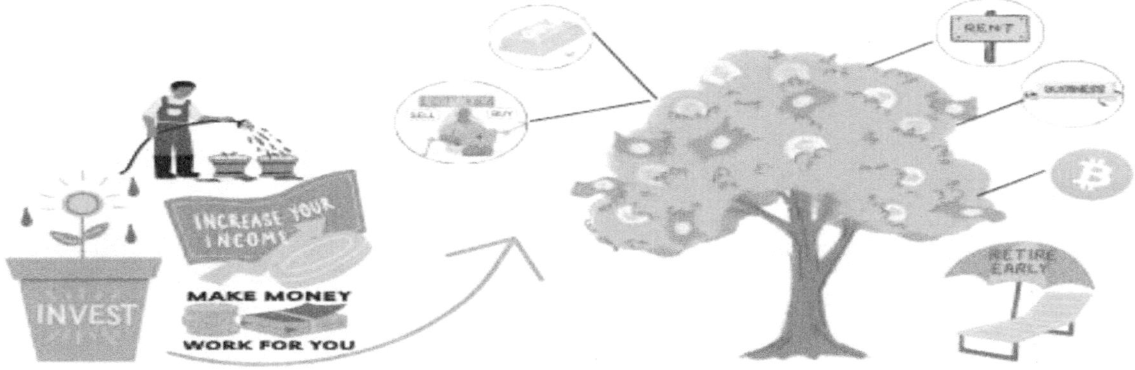

" Lend Where Your Gold Can Come Back Be wise with your money "-
The Richest Man in Babylon [Book]

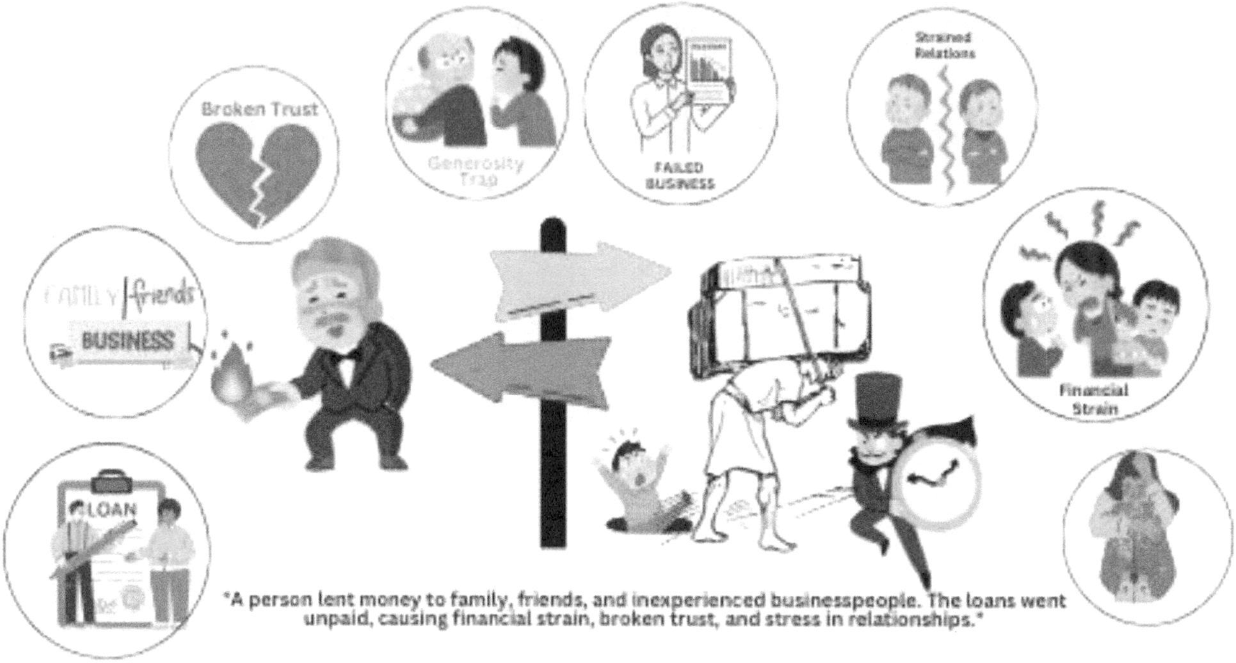

"Gold and silver and copper are not the only forms of money. Money is anything that men accept as a medium of exchange" -
(Clason 12)

" Entertainment is secondary. Focus on beneficial habits—replace distractions like social media with healthy actions such as eating well. Change takes time, but its impact will show " -
(KS)

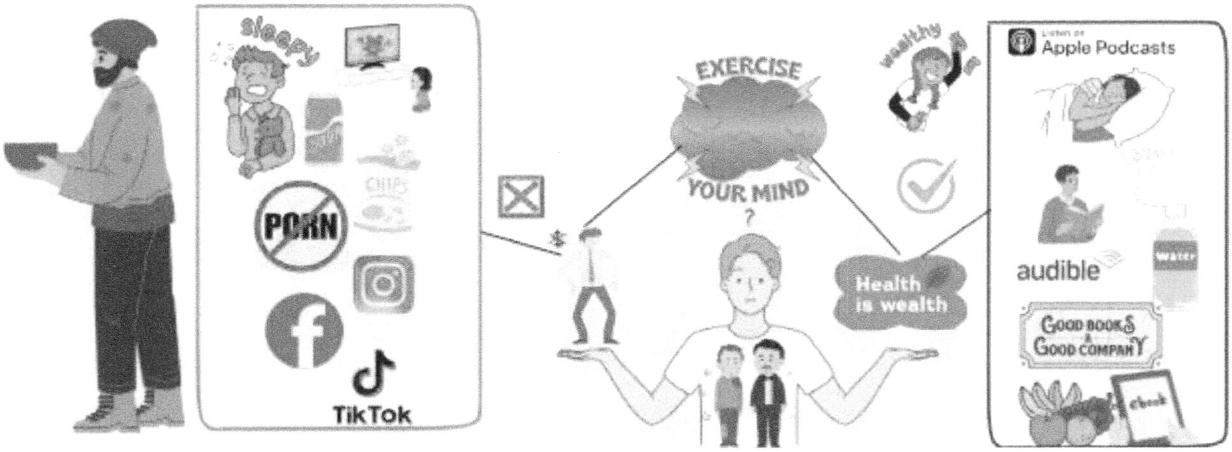

" Failure Can't Cope with persistence " -
Napoleon Hill

" **Most** Powerful force **in the world is** compound interest **"-**
Albert Einstein

" Money **is like** oxygen **you** need **it to breathe but it does** not **guarantee** happiness **"-**
Zig Ziglar

" The lack of money is root to all evil "-
Mark Twain

" A wise person should have money in their head not in their heart "-
Jonathan Swift

"Money **is a terrible** master **but an excellent** servant "- P.T. Barnum

CHAPTER 2 – "QUIRKY FACTS"

" **Apple's Tim Cook's compensation grew to $74.6 million in 2024, compared with $63.2 million the prior year** "- annual proxy filing 1-January-25

" **Coles, a major retailer in Australia, to Halt Kitchen Knife Sales Nationwide Following Queensland Incident where a staff member was stabbed in the back** " - ABC NEWS 15-JAN-2025

" Open AI Faces Copyright Lawsuit in India. Indian book publishers and their international counterparts have filed a copyright lawsuit against Open AI in New Delhi. The lawsuit seeks to restrict the ChatGPT chatbot from accessing proprietary content, adding to the growing number of global legal challenges faced by the AI company " -

OUTLOOK BUSINESS 27-JAN-2025

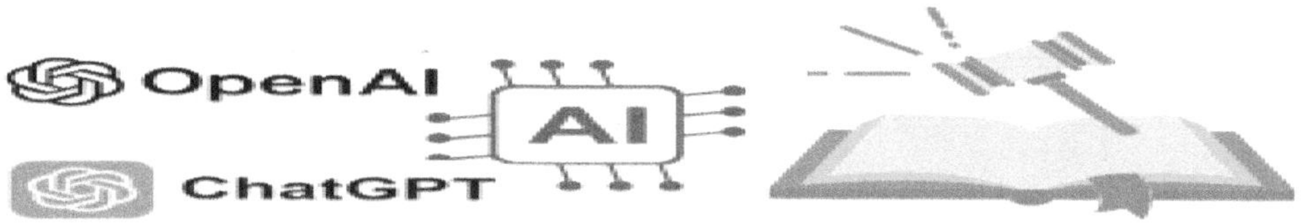

" China's AI Model 'Deep Seek' Challenges U.S. AI Leadership" -

- Deep Seek, poses a **serious challenge** to U.S. dominance in artificial intelligence.
- Deep seek has **outperformed** leading U.S. models like OpenAI's GPT-4 and Meta's Llama 3.1 in benchmark with exceptional performance in problem-solving, mathematics, and coding.
- Deep Seek signals a shift in global AI innovation **and raises concerns** about the United States maintaining its competitive edge.

" Nvidia sheds almost $600 billion in market cap, biggest one-day loss in U.S. history- " -

- The **17% stock** plunge was triggered by concerns over competition from China's AI model, **Deep Seek**, and its potential impact on Nvidia's dominance in the **AI chip market**. [27–JAN -2025]
- Its market capitalization **dropped** from $1.8 trillion to $1.2 trillion.

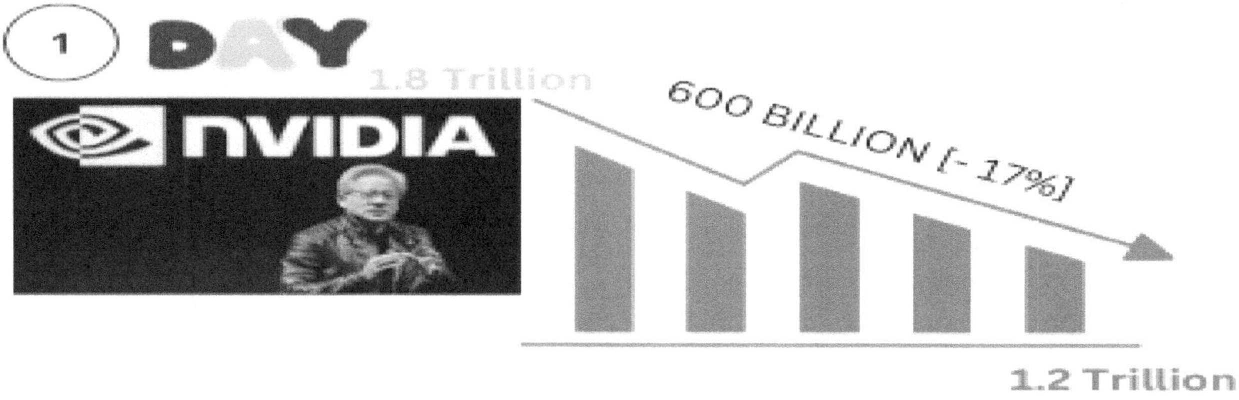

" Microsoft Integrates Deep Seek AI into Windows Co-pilot+ PCs " – According to Microsoft's official blog post

- The company is **bringing Deep Seek AI** models **to Windows** Copilot+ PCs.
- These models, optimized for Neural Processing Units (NPUs), will enhance on-device AI capabilities, starting with Snapdragon-powered PCs and expanding to Intel and AMD platforms.

" Indian Finance Ministry Issues Advisory Against AI Tools " -

- On January 29, 2025, the Indian finance ministry urged employees to **avoid** AI tools like ChatGPT and Deep Seek, citing risks to government data confidentiality.
- Similar restrictions have been imposed by countries such as **Australia and Italy** over data security concerns.
- Reports of the advisory surfaced on February 4, just ahead of OpenAI chief Sam Altman's February 5 visit to India to meet it minister.

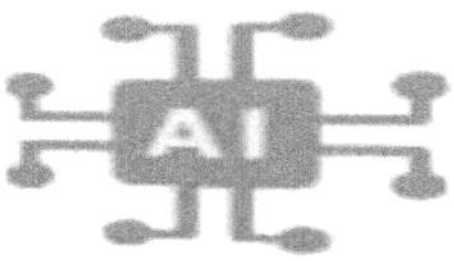

Robotic Doctor: An AI-powered robot named Xiaoyi became the world's first qualified robotic doctor by passing China's medical licensing exams-

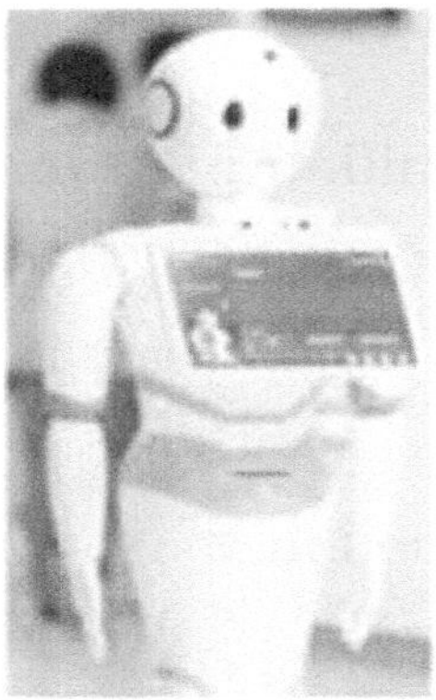
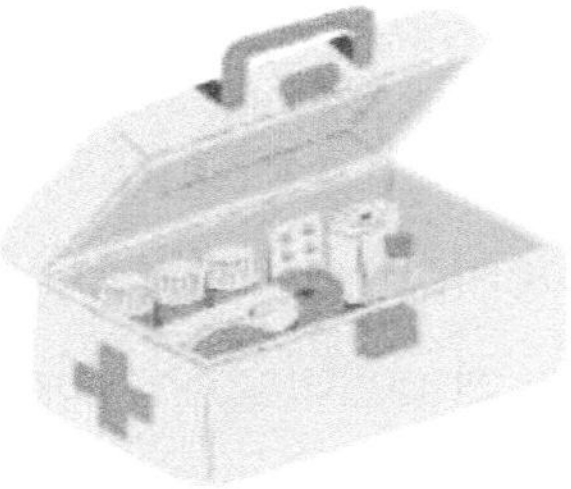

before you climb the LADDER, check it's leaning on the RIGHT WALL.

✦"Australia's Gold Reserve Managed by RBA" -

- The **Reserve Bank of Australia (RBA**) holds approximately 80 tonnes of gold as part of the nation's official reserve assets.
- Gold is Valued at **80 tonnes of gold** valued at **AUD 155 million per tonne**, the total value of the gold reserves would be: $80 \times 155{,}000{,}000 = 12{,}400{,}000{,}000$
- So, the total **worth** of the gold held by the Reserve Bank of Australia is approximately **AUD 12.4 billion**. As of 2024.
- Most of this **gold is stored** at the Bank of England (BoE) in London, the world's largest gold trading hub.

GOLD STORED AT BANK OF ENGLAND

"If current rate of growth of taxation legislation continues, by the end of this century -

- It could reach 830 billion pages.
- It might take 3 million years of continuous reading to fully comprehend.
- Its weight could equal that of 20 aircraft carriers."

Garry Banks, former chairman of the Productivity Commission

PAPER MANUFACTURING FACTORY

Intaxication:- Euphoria @ getting refund from tax office, which lasts until you realise it was your money to start with -

(Author unknown, from Washington post word contest)

Dubai's Tax System Simplified -

No Personal Income Tax: Residents pay no tax on their earnings.

Low Corporate Tax: Businesses are taxed at only **9%** on profits over AED 375,000, with many exemptions in Free Zones.

5% VAT: A small tax applies to most goods and services.

Excise Tax: Higher taxes on harmful products like sugary drinks and tobacco

Business-Friendly: Free Zones offer tax benefits, foreign ownership, and minimal customs duties

"President Donald Trump has ruled out granting Australia a tariff exemption on steel and aluminium exports, with the tariffs set to take effect tomorrow in the United States." - March 2025

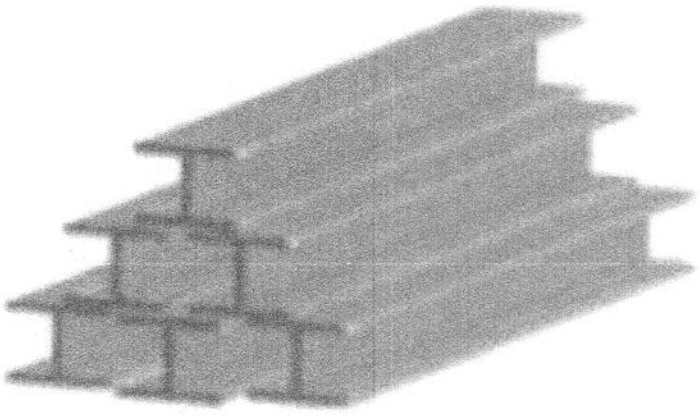

"Tax Deductibility of Body Corporate Fees in Australia " - ATO

- In Australia, body corporate fees are tax deductible in the **year they are incurred** unless designated for capital improvements.
- General-purpose sinking and administration funds are fully deductible, even if allocated for capital investments.

""Borrowing expenses exceeding $100 must be amortised over the shorter of the loan's term or five years. If the loan is repaid early, the remaining expenses can be claimed in that year." -
Australian Taxation Office (ATO

Australian Government

Australian Taxation Office

$$\text{Amortisation expense} = \frac{\text{Cost of intangible asset}}{\text{Useful life}}$$

" In Australia, you can claim 67 cents per hour for home office running costs, covering items like electricity, gas, internet, phone, and stationery " -
Australian Taxation Office (ATO) 2024

(ato)

" New York City, New York, is the richest city in the USA and the world, home to 350,000 millionaires and 60 billionaires." - 2025

"Top 10 Global Economies in 2025 (Nominal GDP):"

1. United States – $30.34 trillion
2. China – $19.53 trillion
3. Germany – $4.92 trillion
4. Japan – $4.39 trillion
5. India – $4.27 trillion
6. United Kingdom – $3.73 trillion
7. France – $3.28 trillion
8. Italy – $2.46 trillion
9. Canada – $2.33 trillion
10. Brazil – $2.31 trillion

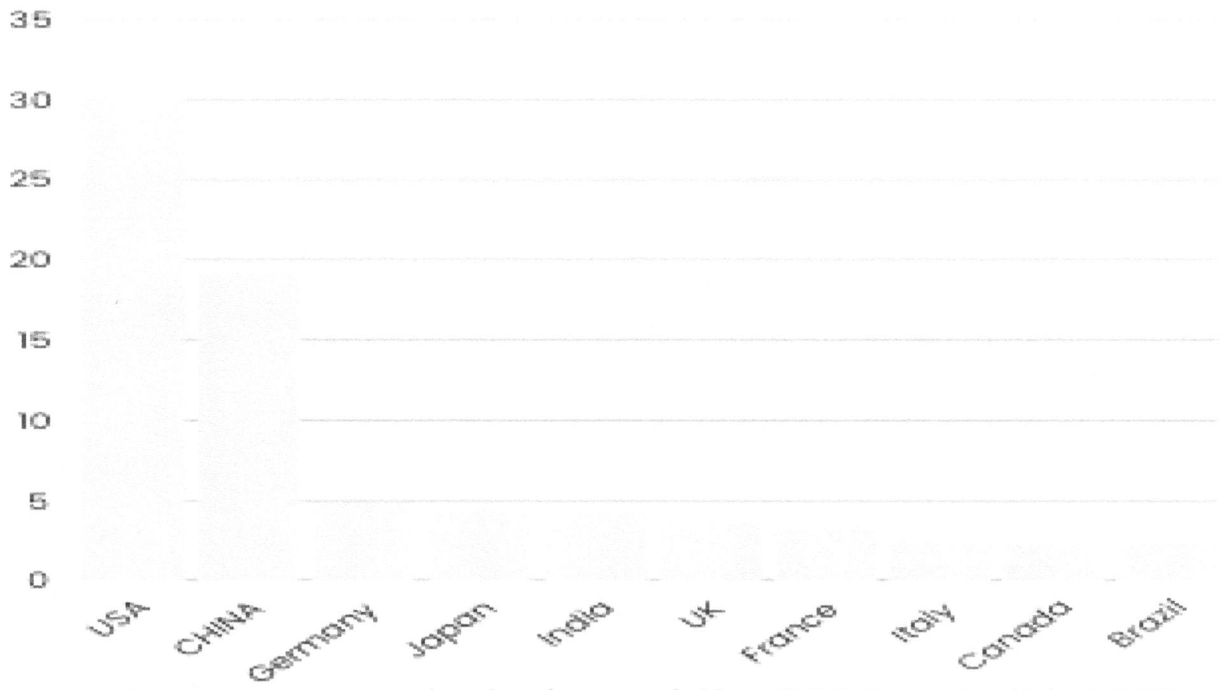

Largest economies in the world by GDP (nominal) in 2025

"Top 10 Global Economies in 2025: Growth Rate Estimates"

1. **United States: ~2.0% annual GDP growth**
2. **China: ~4.5% annual GDP growth**
3. **Germany: ~1.2% annual GDP growth**
4. **Japan: ~1.0% annual GDP growth**
5. **India: ~6.5% annual GDP growth (fastest among major economies)**
6. **United Kingdom: ~1.5% annual GDP growth**
7. **France: ~1.3% annual GDP growth**
8. **Italy: ~0.9% annual GDP growth**
9. **Canada: ~1.8% annual GDP growth**
10. **Brazil: ~2.3% annual GDP growth**

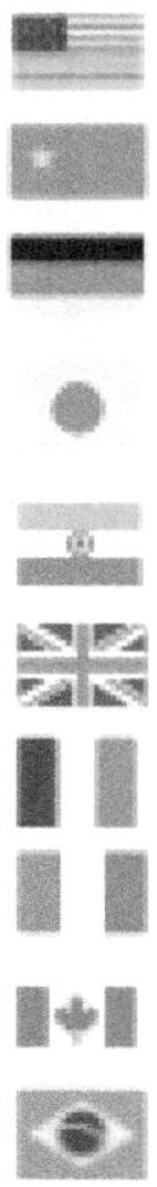

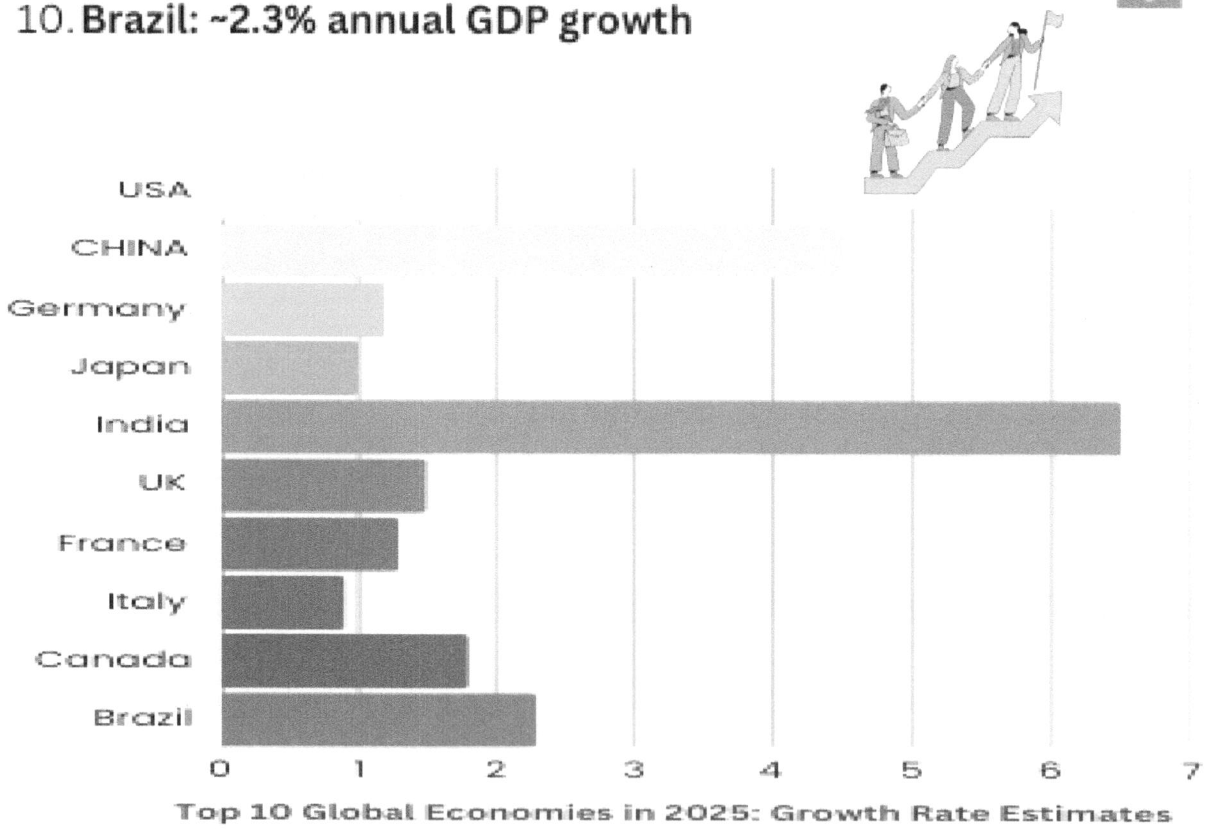

There are 195 countries in the world. This includes: 193 member states of the United Nations (UN). 2 observer states: the Vatican City (Holy See) and Palestine. - 2025

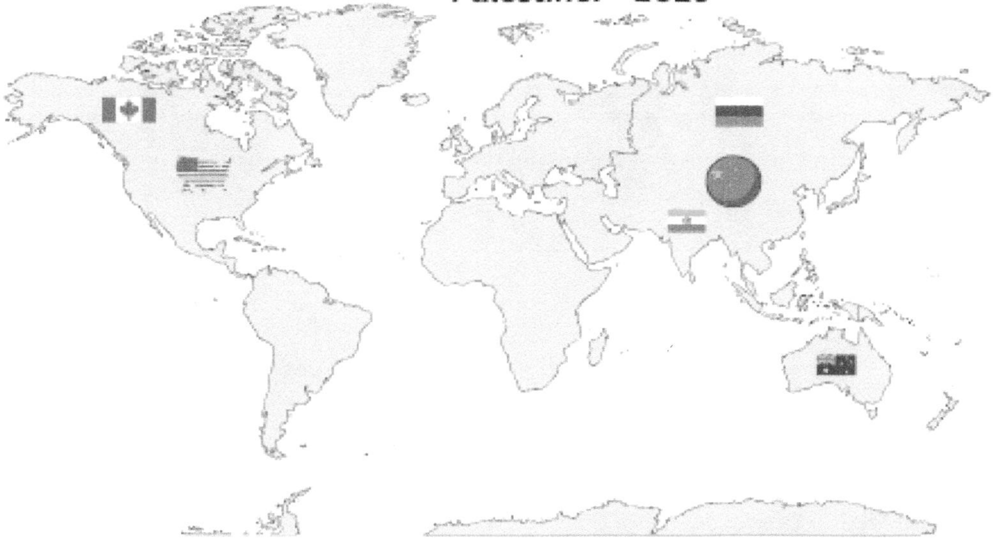

"Man hauls a wheelbarrow of cash for daily groceries."

uniquely quirky

Top 13 countries with the highest inflation rates as of : 2024

1. **Zimbabwe: 635%**
2. **Argentina: 229%**
3. **Sudan: 200%**
4. **South Sudan Republic: 120.6%**
5. **Türkiye (Republic of Turkey): 60.9%**
6. **Venezuela: 59.6%**
7. **Central Asia and the Caucasus: 38.7%**
8. **Sierra Leone: 36.6%**
9. **Egypt: 33.3%**
10. **Nigeria: 32.26%**
11. **Iran: 31.7%**
12. **Malawi: 30.6%**
13. **Angola: 28.4%**

DATA SOURCE - www.imf.org/external/datamapper

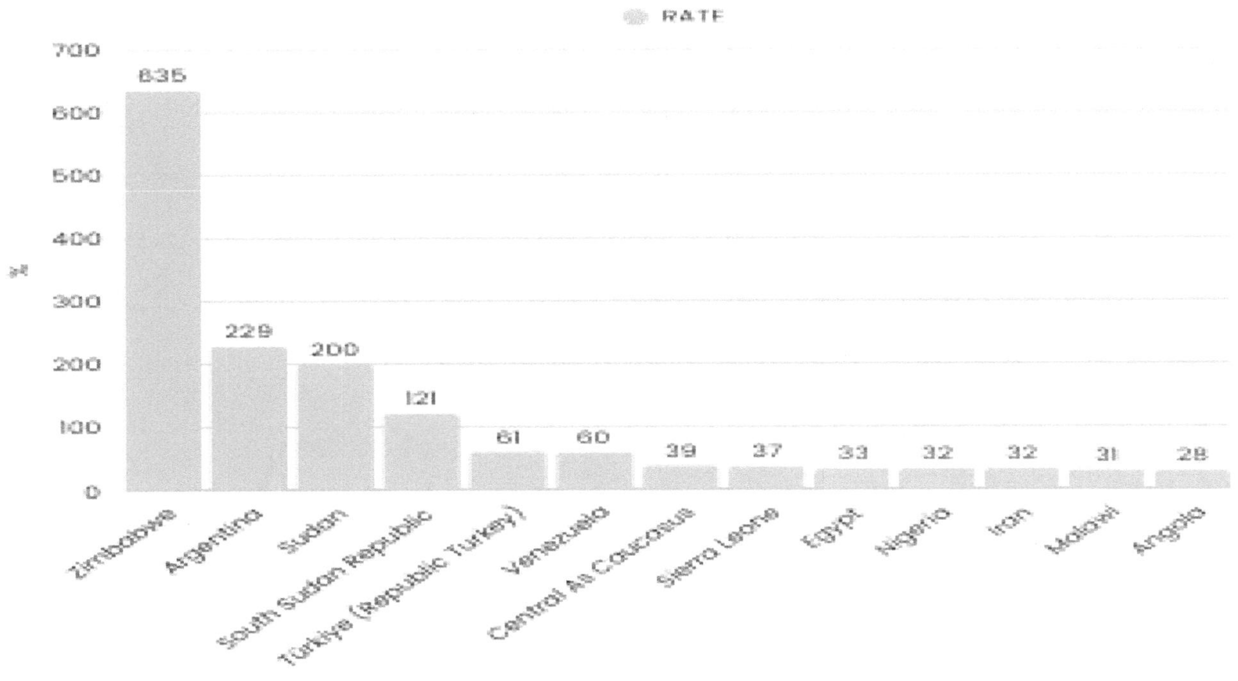

HIGHES INFLATION RATES – SOURCE WWW.IMF.ORG

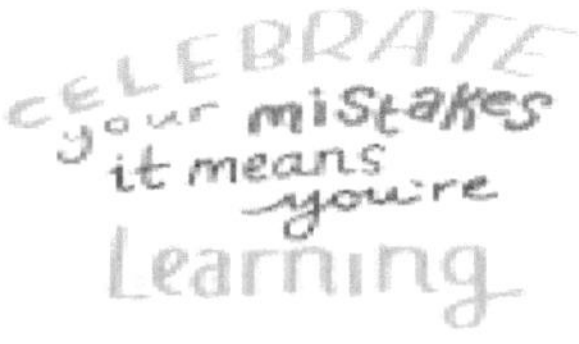

"High Inflation Hotspot: Zimbabwe"

Economy

- The **Zimbabwean Dollar (ZWL)** is the official currency, but the **US Dollar (USD)** is widely used for transactions.
- The government allows the **dual-currency system** to stabilize the economy, although it promotes the use of ZWL.
- USD is acquired through remittances, exports, savings, tourism, and informal markets

Key income sources for the government include -

- Mining (gold, platinum, diamonds, chrome)
- Agriculture (tobacco, cotton, sugar, maize)
- Tourism (Victoria Falls, wildlife reserves)
- Taxes (income, VAT, corporate)
- Customs and trade fees
- Foreign aid and loans

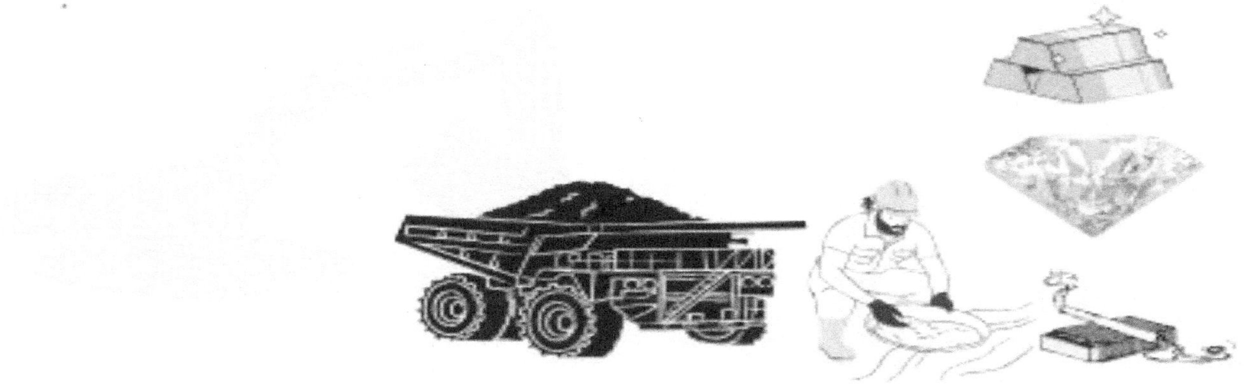

Inflation & Interest Rates - 

- Zimbabwe's inflation rate is exceptionally high, estimated **at 635%** (according to the IMF).

- Due to past **hyperinflation**, **USD** remains a preferred and stable **currency** for many citizens.

Zimbabwe's inflation rate surges to 231,000,000% IN 2008

Wealth and Resources -

Strive Masiyiwa is Zimbabwe's **richest person**, with an estimated net worth of USD **$1.8–$1.9 billion**, largely from **telecommunications** and **renewable energy** ventures.

Daily Life and Currency Use -

Many stores and vendors price goods in USD, while smaller-scale transactions may still use ZWL.

Food prices (approximate in ZWL): -

Bread (loaf): ~28.50 ZWL
Cooking oil (2L): ~113 ZWL
Milk (1L): ~43 ZWL
Mealie-meal (10kg): ~299 ZWL

Better
Days
AHEAD

"Daily Inflation Hall of Fame for the Century"

1 **"Hungary (1946): Prices doubled every 15 hours, with daily inflation rates exceeding 207%"**

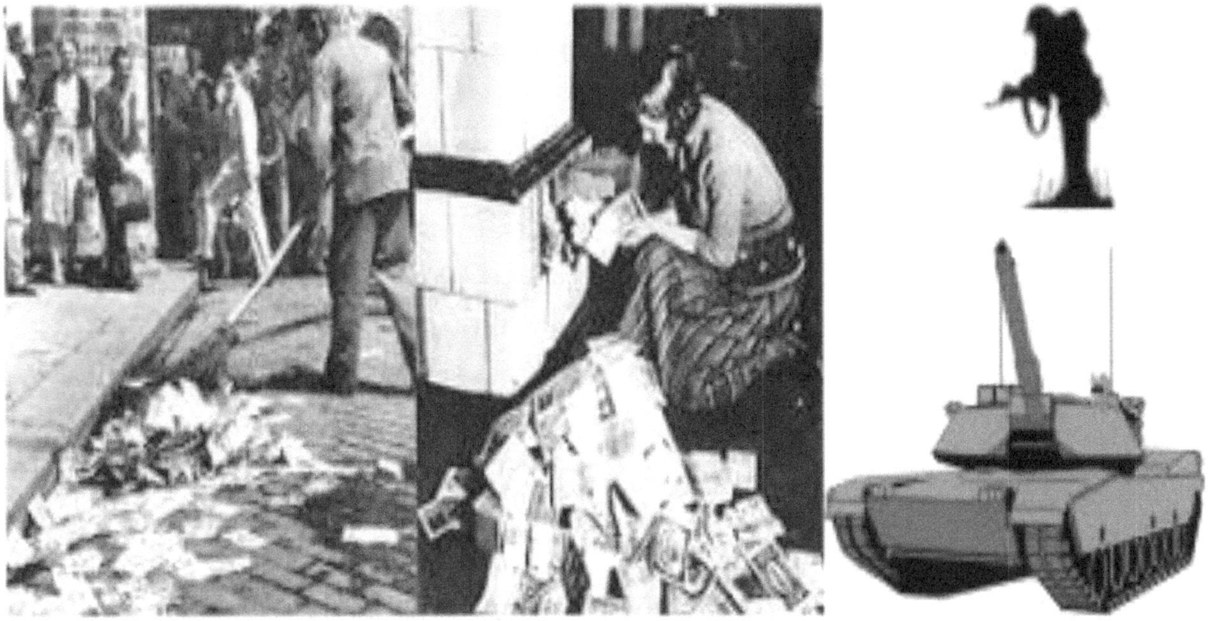

1946 HYPERINFLATION IN HUNGARY DUE TO WORLD WAR 2

2 "Zimbabwe (2008): Prices doubled every 24 hours, with daily inflation around 98%"

"A man rushes to pay his fare before boarding, knowing it will double by the time he reaches his destination."

LEARNING is a CONTINUOUS LIFESTYLE

3 "Germany (1923): Prices doubled every 3.7 days, with daily inflation approximately 20.9%."

Weimar government's main crisis occurred in 1923 after the Germans missed a reparations. payment late in 1922

④ "Greece (1944): Prices doubled every 4.3 days, with daily inflation about 18.9% "

The hyperinflation incident in Greece was largely caused by World War II debt

5 "China (1949): Prices doubled approximately every 5 days, with daily inflation estimated around 14.7% "

China abandoned the traditional silver standard, in response to deflation caused by rising silver prices, and introduced its own paper currency

Sometimes
TURNING UP
is enough.

6 "Venezuela (2018): **Daily inflation reached** up to 4% **during its hyperinflation crisis."**

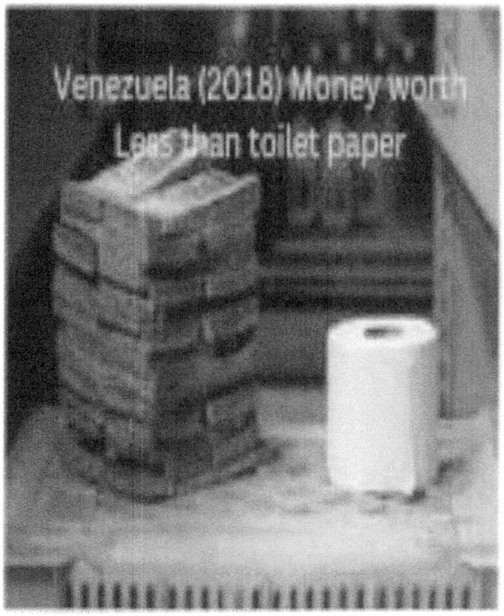

Several factors contributed to Venezuela's hyperinflation, including years of economic mismanagement, reliance on oil revenues, and corruption.

Grateful

7 "Argentina (1989): Daily inflation peaked at 3%, with prices doubling every few weeks."

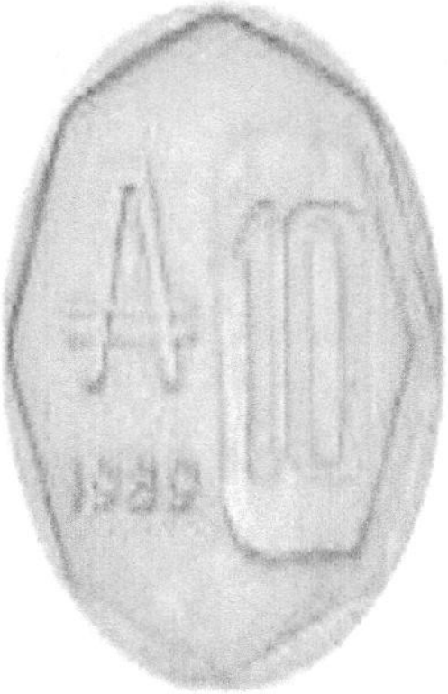

The central government, hampered by low tax collections and desperate for revenues, turned to the central bank for finance through the taxation of deposits and money creation. Inflation, which had risen gradually over the previous three decades, soared—reaching average annual rates of 2,600 percent in 1989 and 1990.

8 "Poland (1923): **Inflation reached a** daily rate of 2.5%, **with significant instability after World War I."**

In order to pay the striking workers the government simply printed more money. This flood of money led to hyperinflation

"Yugoslavia (1994): Prices doubled every 1.4 days, translating to 64.6% daily inflation during the peak month."

hyperinflation was fueled by an explosive growth in the money supply, which was used to finance government deficits and military expenditures.

10 "Brazil (1980s–1990s): Daily inflation often hovered around 2%, with chronic inflationary pressures."

-

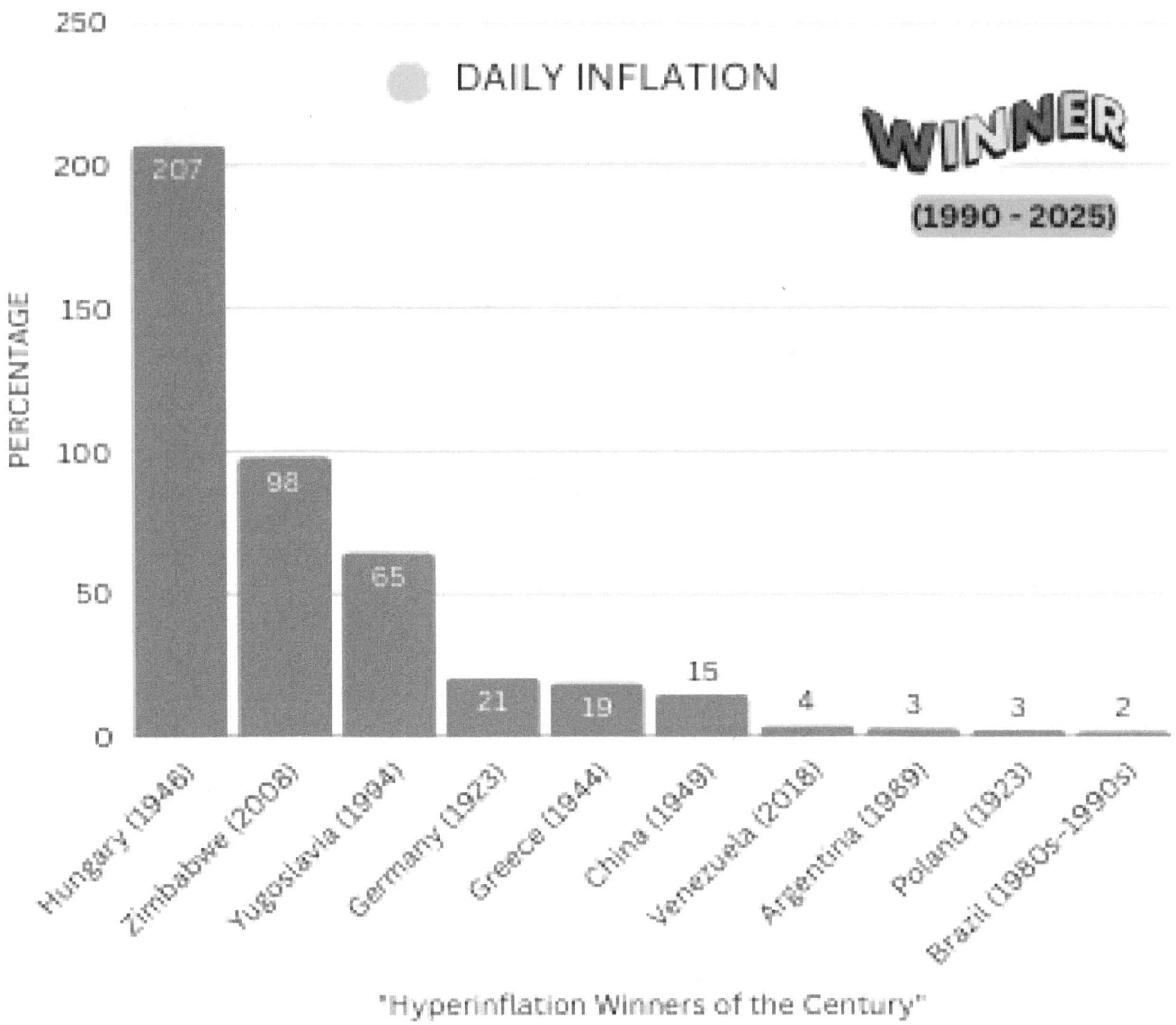

DAILY INFLATION
WINNER
(1990 - 2025)
PERCENTAGE
250
200
150
100
50
0
207
98
65
21
19
15
4
3
3
2
Hungary (1946)
Zimbabwe (2008)
Yugoslavia (1994)
Germany (1923)
Greece (1944)
China (1949)
Venezuela (2018)
Argentina (1989)
Poland (1923)
Brazil (1980s-1990s)
"Hyperinflation Winners of the Century"

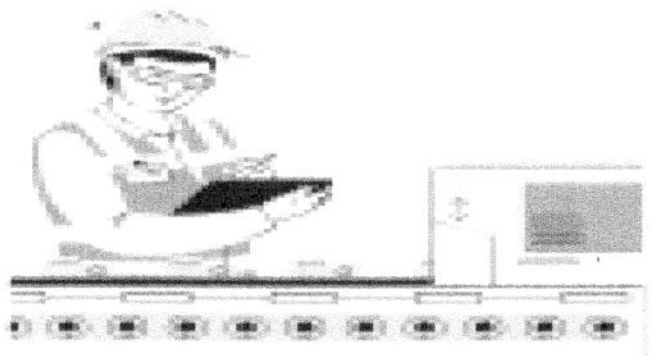

DEFLATION

COUNTRY	INFLATION RATE (%) ↑	DATE MEASURED
Afghanistan	-6.7%	08/24
Sri Lanka	-0.8%	10/24
Costa Rica	-0.8%	10/24
Bahamas	-0.5%	07/24
Brunei	-0.4%	09/24
Panama	-0.3%	10/24
Senegal	-0.2%	10/24
El Salvador	-0.1%	10/24
Djibouti	-0.1%	09/24

worldpopulationreview.com

Deflation Causes:

Deflation can be driven by various factors, including:

- Increased **productivity** and an **abundance** of goods and services.
- A **decrease** in total or aggregate **demand**.
- A decrease in the **supply of money** and credit.

Potential Effects:

- **Short-term relief**: Falling prices benefit consumers initially.
- **Economic challenges**: Prolonged deflation can hurt growth.
- **Less spending**: People delay purchases, reducing economic activity.
- **Higher debt burden**: Debt becomes harder to repay, risking defaults and financial instability.

Deflationary Trap:

In some cases, expected deflation can lead to further economic weakness, potentially creating a "deflationary trap" where the economy becomes stuck in a cycle of declining prices and reduced activity.

Great Depression (1929–1939)

Some notable examples of deflationary traps in history:

1. **The Great Depression (1929–1939)**: The U.S. experienced a severe deflationary spiral during this period. Falling prices led to reduced production, widespread unemployment, and decreased consumer spending, deepening the economic crisis.
2. **Japan's Lost Decade (1990s)**: After the asset bubble burst, Japan faced prolonged deflation. Consumers delayed spending, expecting further price drops, which hindered economic recovery for years.
3. **Eurozone Debt Crisis (2010s)**: Countries like Greece and Spain experienced deflationary pressures due to austerity measures, leading to reduced economic activity and high unemployment.

Japan asset bubble burst

Eurozone Debt Crisis (2010s)

One day AT A time

Top Countries With Lowest Inflation 2024

	COUNTRY	INFLATION RATE (%) ↑	DATE MEASURED
	Papua New Guinea	0.1%	06/24
	Timor Leste	0.2%	10/24
	China	0.3%	10/24
	Georgia	0.3%	10/24
	Lithuania	0.3%	10/24
	Bahrain	0.4%	09/24
	Trinidad and Tobag	0.4%	09/24
	Rwanda	0.5%	10/24
	Switzerland	0.6%	10/24
	Armenia	0.6%	10/24

DATA SOURCE - worldpopulationreview.com -

"Top 10 Countries with the Highest Interest Rates - (January 2025)"

Bank of Russia

BANCO CENTRAL DO BRASIL

Bank of England

UNITED STATES FEDERAL RESERVE SYSTEM

RESERVE BANK OF AUSTRALIA

中国人民银行
THE PEOPLE'S BANK OF CHINA

BANK OF CANADA

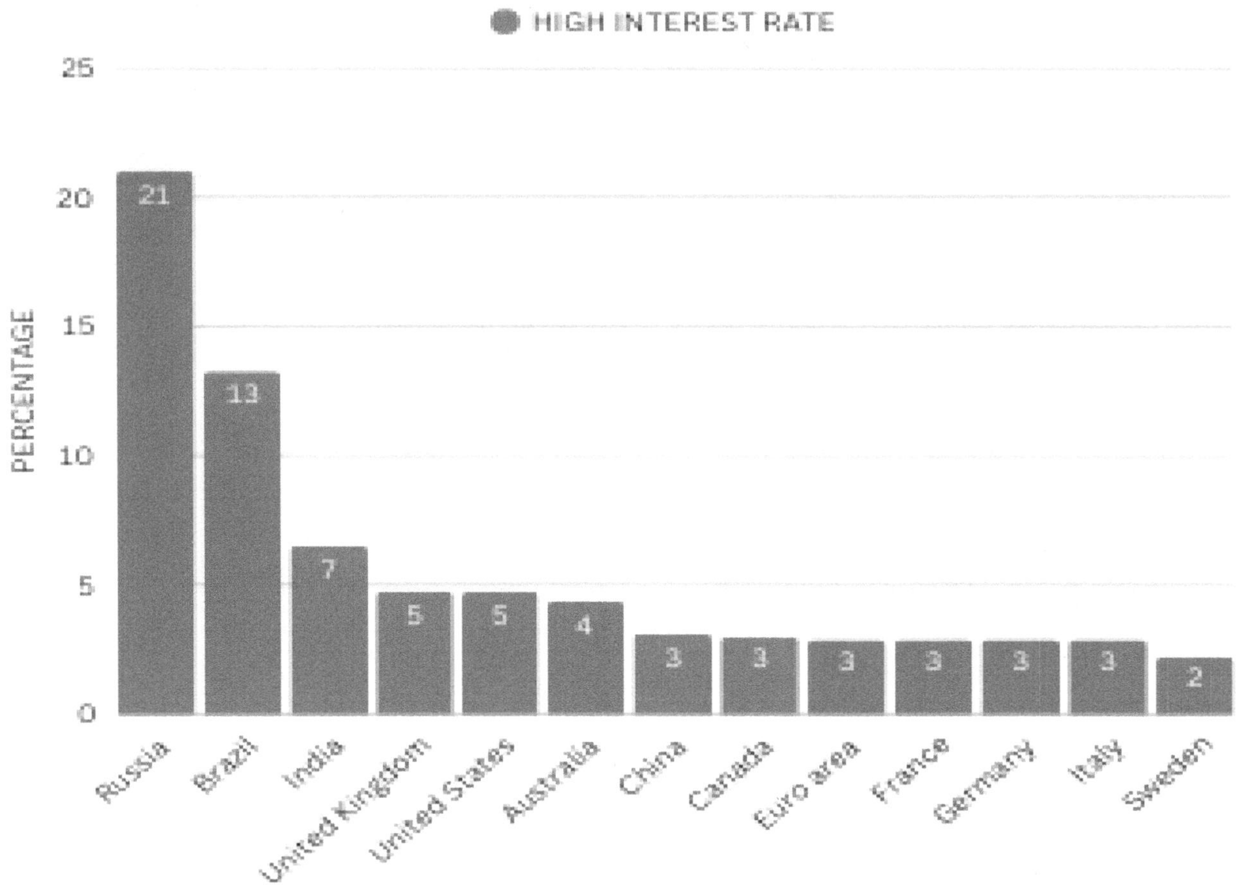

"Top 10 Countries with the Highest Interest Rates - (January 2025)"

"Top 10 countries with most gold reserves - 2024 "

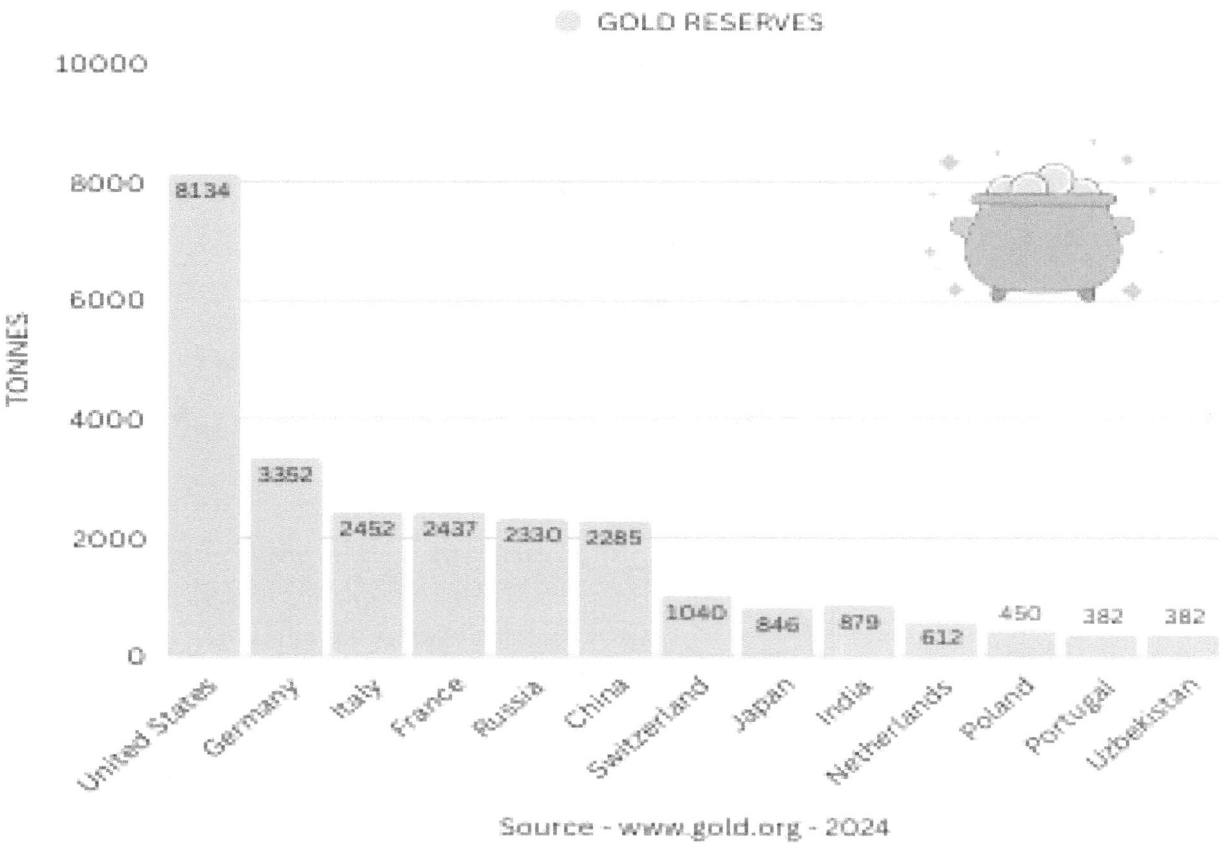

"Things moved offline to online last 20 years,"

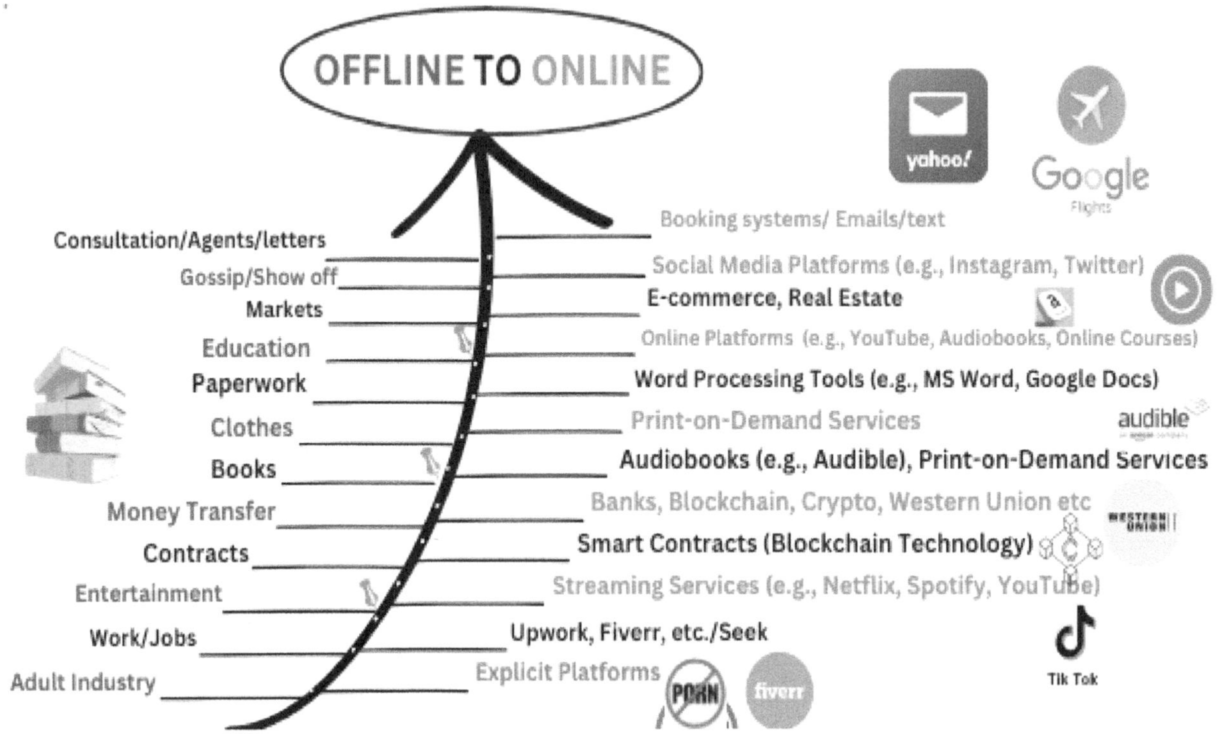

Pornography addiction

Behavioral disorder

Pornography addiction is the scientifically controversial application of an addiction model to the use of pornography. Pornography use may be part of compulsive behavior, with negative consequences to one's physical, mental, social, or financial well-being.

Source: Wikipedia

Less ^

CHAPTER 3 - "THINK BIG: HOW FAR DOES GENIUS GO?"

Answers can be found on the following pages. Feel free to use the provided answer sections to record your responses as you work through the questions.

How much is the total value of Russia's natural resources estimated to be? USD

A) $25 trillion

B) $50 trillion

C) $75 trillion

D) $100 trillion.

ANSWER -

What is the estimated storage capacity of the human brain?

a) 1 terabyte

b) 2.5 petabytes

c) 500 gigabytes

d) 1 petabyte

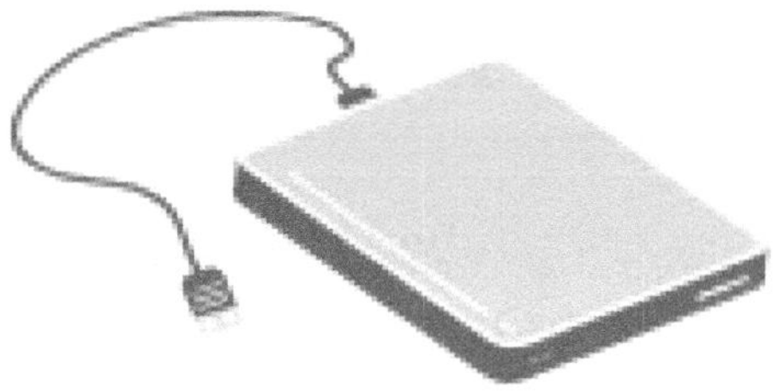

ANSWER -

IT TAKES A
big heart
TO HELP SHAPE
little minds.

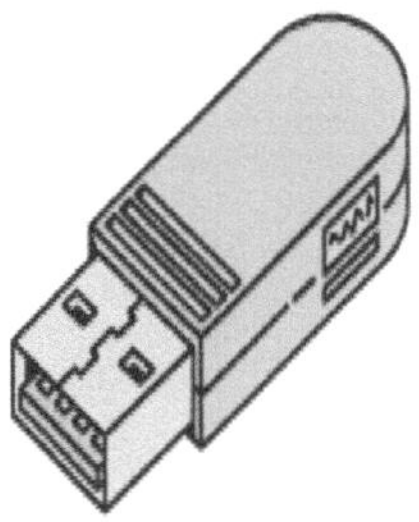

How many hours of TV shows are the brain's storage capacity equivalent to?

a) 1 million hours

b) 2 million hours

c) 3 million hours

d) 4 million hours.

ANSWER -

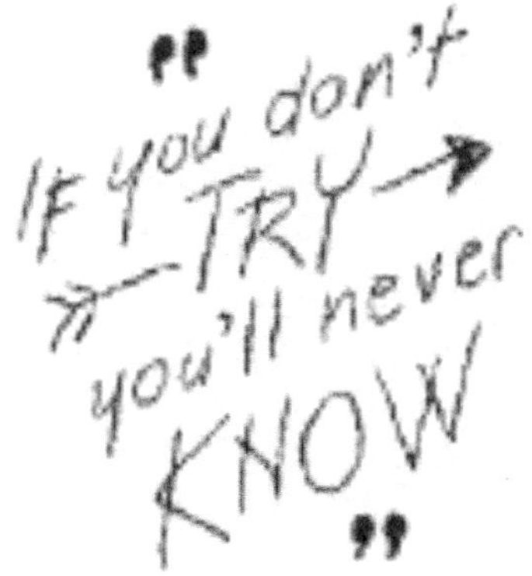

ANSWERS SHEET -

"Russia's natural resources "

√ Russia's natural resources are estimated to be worth between $75 trillion and $100 trillion

This immense wealth comes from its **vast reserves of oil, natural gas, coal**, precious metals, and **other minerals**.

HUMAN BRAIN

The storage capacity of the human brain is estimated to be around 2.5 petabytes, which is roughly equivalent to 2.5 million gigabytes.

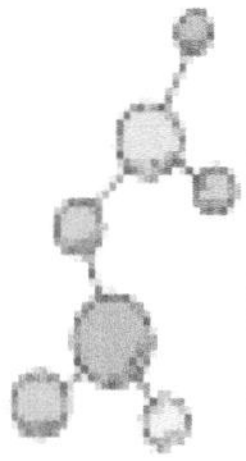

This immense capacity comes from the brain's incredible network of neurons, with trillions of connections (synapses) working together to store and process information

To put that into perspective, it's like having a digital video recorder (DVR) capable of storing about 3 million hours of TV shows. You could keep watching continuously for over 300 years without running out of space!

CHAPTER 4 – "INVESTMENT ANALYSIS: GAINS, LOSSES, AND LESSONS?"

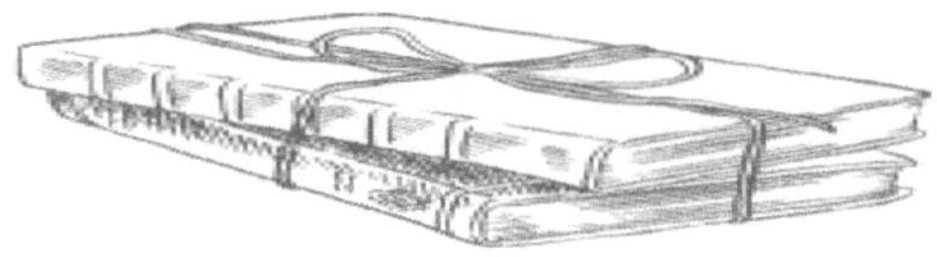

"A $19,672 USD Investment in Bajaj Finance Back in 2012"

"Imagine you invested $19,672 USD in Bajaj Finance back in 2012. What would you expect today?

- A) A modest return
- B) A life-changing fortune
- C) A break-even scenario
- D) A loss of value"

"Let's Dive In" -

Background – Bajaj Finance is a non-banking financial company in India, started in 1996 and focused on lending.

Numbers Breakdown - Bajaj Finance Limited (BFL) had its Initial Public Offering (IPO) listed on the stock exchanges on 1996.

- **Listing Date:** November 19, 2010
- **Stock Exchanges:** BFL is listed on both the Bombay Stock Exchange (BSE) and the National Stock Exchange (NSE).

Lump Sum Investment: A single investment of $19,672 made all at once.

SIP Investments: Investments made in small increments over a period.

BAJAJ FINANCE

** "Applied: Avg. 54 INR/USD (2012) & 83 INR/USD (2025)."

Lump Sum investment – Considering no shares sold share till 2024.

Exchanged $19,672 invested in March 2012 amounts to 1,003,272 INR, buying **12540** shares at 80 INR each

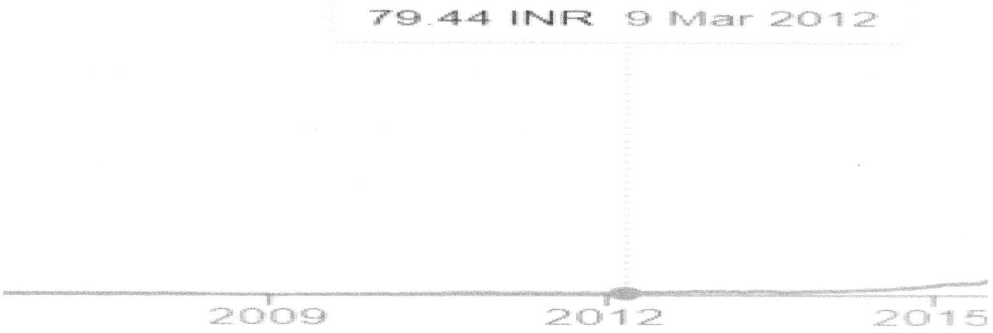

Share Splits: Due to the appreciation of Bajaj Finance's share price and exponential growth in its underlying business, the board has initiated **several share splits** to maintain higher liquidity.

- 2013 share split: 1: 1.02936 (1.02 shares for every 1 held).
- 2017 share split: 1:10 (10 shares for every 1 held).

Let's examine how these splits have impacted the investment –

2013 – 1.02 x 12540 = **12,920 shares** (rounded to the nearest whole share).

2017 – 10 x 37620 = **129,200**

During previous year 2016-17, pursuant to approval of the Members -

(i) Authorised share capital of the Company was increased and subdivided from ₹75 crore consisting of 75,000,000 equity shares of face value of ₹10 each to ₹150 crore consisting of 750,000,000 equity shares of face value of ₹2 each, consequent to the decision to subdivide issued capital of 53,872,190 equity shares of face value of ₹10 each as on the record date i.e. 10 September 2016 (end of the day), into 269,360,950 equity shares of face value of ₹2 each and declaration of bonus shares as stated in (ii) below.

(ii) On 14 September 2016, the Allotment Committee of the Board of Directors allotted 269,360,950 equity shares of face value of ₹2 each as bonus shares in the proportion of one bonus equity share for every one equity share of face value of ₹2 held as on the record date, by capitalising an amount of ₹538,721,900 from securities premium account. The bonus shares were listed on BSE Ltd. and National Stock Exchange of India Ltd. w.e.f. 19 September 2016. Other than this, Company has not allotted any bonus shares in previous years.

"EXCERPT FROM 2018 ANNUAL REPORT."

Let's examine how these splits have impacted the investment –

2013 – 1.02 x 12540 = **12,920 shares** (rounded to the nearest whole share).

2017 – 10 x 37620 = **129,200**

By 2017, the shares would total 129,200 shares.

The share price in March 2025 is approximately **INR 8,870.**

The total investment value =

129,200 shares × 8,870 = INR **1,148,284,000.**

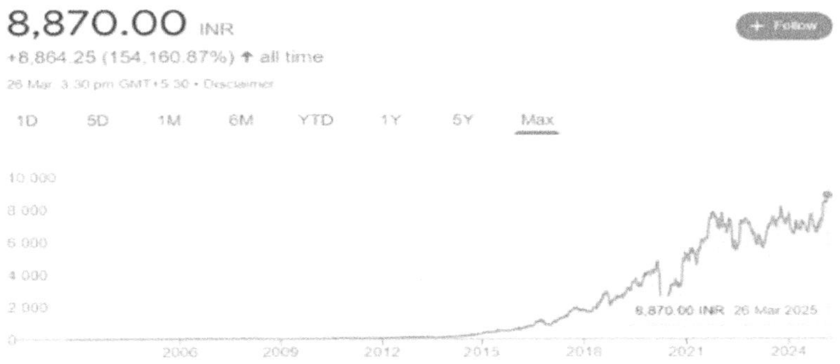

Share price on march 2025 -

Converted to USD at today's exchange rate:

INR 1,148,284,000 × 0.012 = **$13,407,484.**

"Hold on—we haven't factored in dividends yet! Let's calculate their contribution since 2012. Note: Dividends are subject to tax, which is not included."

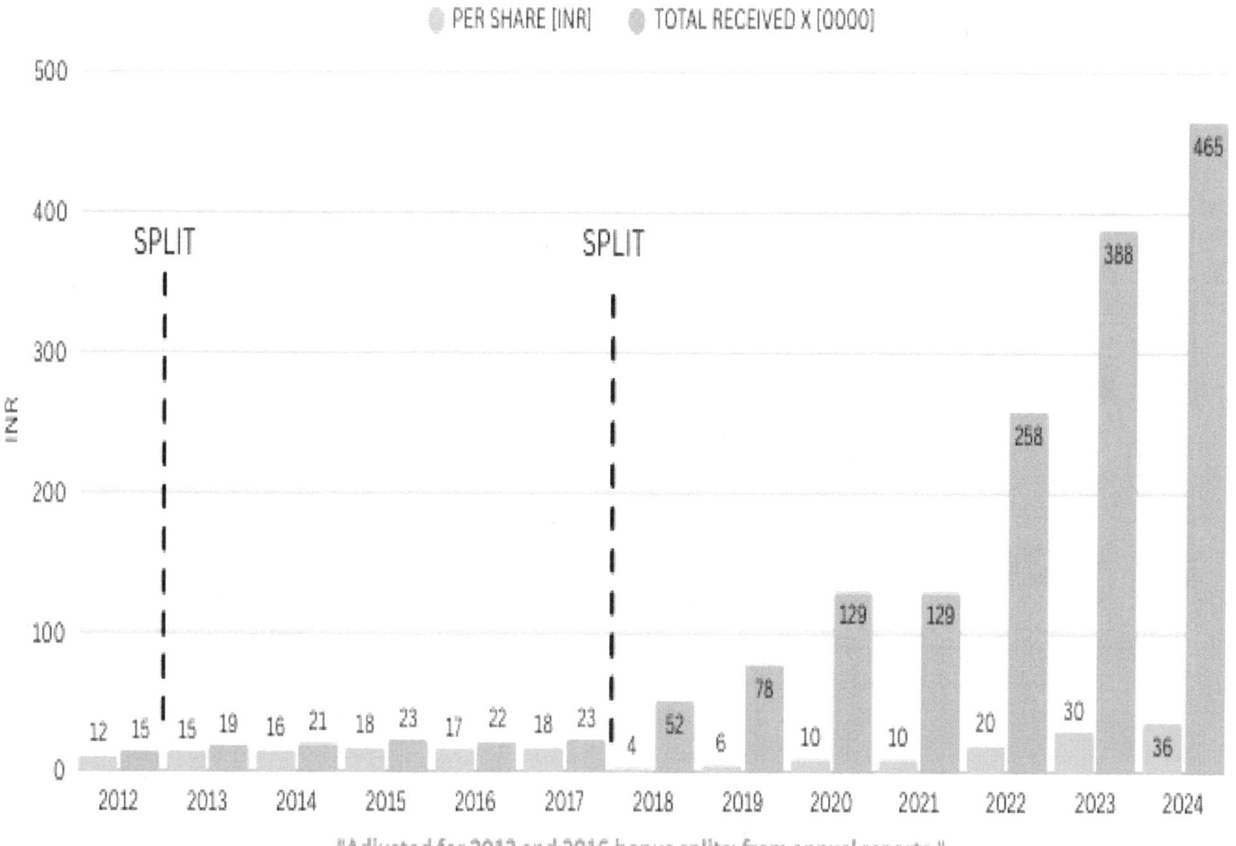

"Adjusted for 2013 and 2016 bonus splits; from annual reports."

"**Total dividends [2012 – 2024]** = 150,480 + 193,800 + 206,720 + 232,560 + 219,640 + 232,560 + 516,800 + 77,520 + 1,292,000 + 1,292,000 + 2,584,000 + 3,876,000 + 4,651,200 = **INR 15,525,280**"

Converted to USD = $ 181096.80

Investment value + Dividend = **$13,407,484 + $ 181096.80 = $13,588,580.80**

"Therefore, the $19,672 invested in March 2012 has grown to $13.5 million by March 2025, over a span of 13 years."

IPHONE INVESTING –

iPhone: Apple is a U.S.-based brand that manufactures iPhones and other electronics.

Apple was **founded** in 1976.

Apple was listed on the **stock exchange** in 1980.

The **first iPhone** came onto the market in 2007.

People line up to buy new iPhones, showcasing the incredible **brand loyalty**.

Steve Jobs requires no introduction; his visionary leadership shaped the tech world.

"YOUR BRAND IS WHAT OTHER PEOPLE SAY ABOUT YOU WHEN YOU'RE NOT IN THE ROOM."

Man Rushing to Buy new iPhone Launched

If you're an iPhone fan who **buys a new iPhone** at each launch, let's see:

- How much money have you **spent** so far??
- The returns you could have made if you'd invested the same amount in **Apple stock** at each launch.? (Note: Prices may vary slightly by location.)

SHOP NOW

Original iPhone (2007) – Priced at $499

iPhone 3G (2008): $199 (8GB)
, $299 (16GB)

iPhone 3GS (2009): $199 (16GB),
$299 (32GB)

iPhone 4 (2010) – $199 (16GB)
and $299 (32GB)

iPhone 4S (2011) – $199 (16GB), $299 (32GB), and $399 (64GB)

iPhone 5 (2012): $199 (subsidized), $649 (unlocked)

iPhone 5S (2013): $199 (subsidized), $649 (unlocked)

iPhone 6 (2014): $649

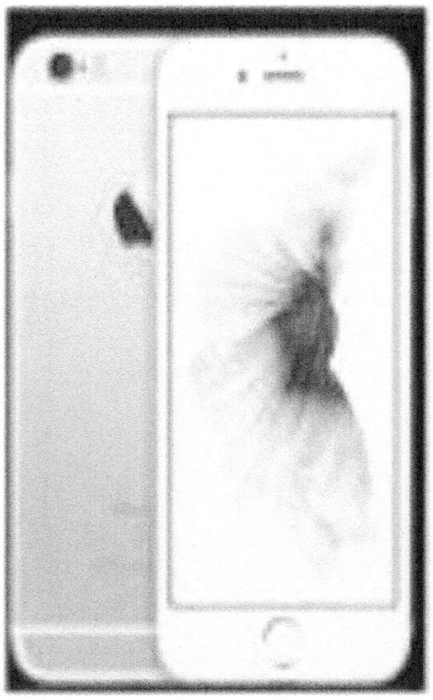

iPhone 6S (2015): $649

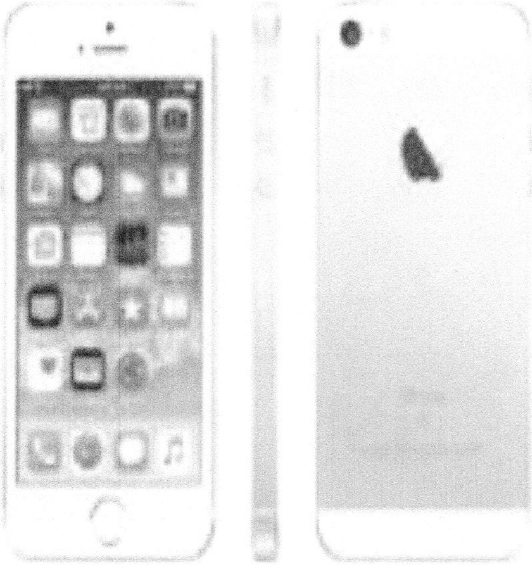

iPhone SE (1st Gen) 2016
$399

iPhone 7 (2016): $649

iPhone X (2017): $999

iPhone XS (2018): $999

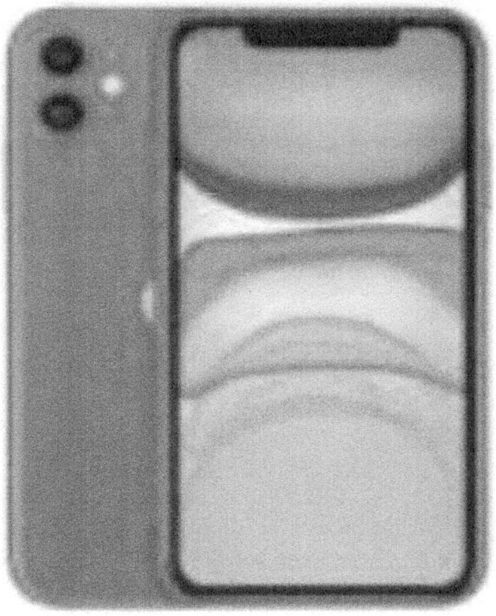

iPhone 11 (2019): $699

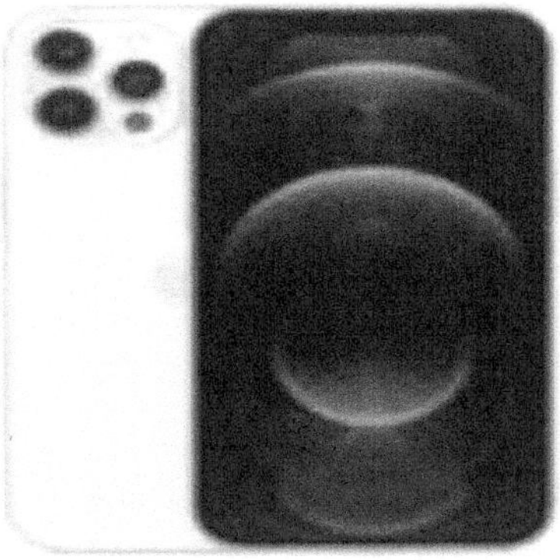

iPhone 12 Pro Max (2020): $1,099

iPhone 13 Pro Max 2021 $1,099

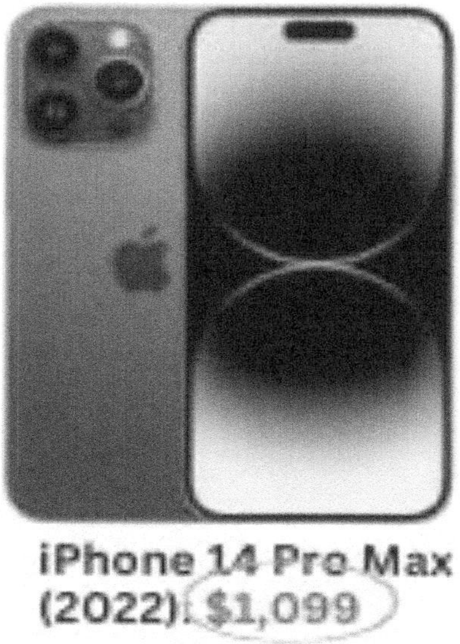

** **Apple launches** multiple iPhone models each year. To simplify calculations, we have **focused** only on the most **expensive mode**l launched each year, and all **prices** listed are in United States dollars.

Let's calculate the **total cost** of all the new iPhone models **purchased at each launch** from **2007 to 2024** -

$499 + 299 + 299 + 299 + 399 + 649 + 649 + 649 + 649 + 649 + 999 + 999 + 699 + 1099 +1099 + 1099 +1199 + 1199 = **$ 13,432**

An iPhone **enthusiast** would have **spent** approximately **$13,432** on all the **launches** so far.

INVEST!

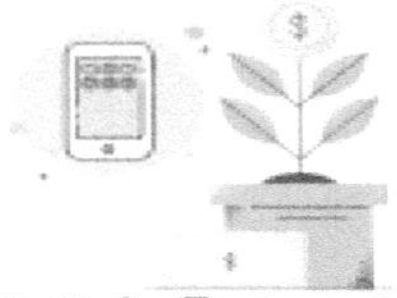

" IF IPHONES WERE STOCKS: $13,432 IN APPLE INC. "

What If You Had Invested $13,432 Instead?

Take a guess—how much do you think it would be worth today?

A. $30,000
B. $60,000
C. $600,000
D. or another amount?

Write your answer in the box below.

ANSWER -

Investor Relations

Dividend amounts not split adjusted.

Declared	Record	Payable	Amount	Type
January 30, 2025	February 10, 2025	February 13, 2025	$0.25	Regular Cash
October 31, 2024	November 11, 2024	November 14, 2024	$0.25	Regular Cash
August 1, 2024	August 12, 2024	August 15, 2024	$0.25	Regular Cash

"Excerpt from the Apple website"

r.apple.com/faq/default.aspx

Store Mac iPad iPhone Watch AirPods TV & Home Entertainment Accessories Support

Investor Relations

Stock Price SEC Filings Leadership and Governance Our Values FAQ Co

How many times has Apple's stock split?

Apple's stock has split five times since the company went public. The stock split on a 4-for-1 basis on August 28, 2020, a 7-for-1 basis on June 9, 2014, and split on a 2-for-1 basis on February 28, 2005, June 21, 2000, and June 16, 1987.

"Excerpt from the Apple website"

Now that we've imagined investing the total amount, let's break it down further by considering each iPhone purchase as an individual investment. How would these smaller amounts have grown over time?

Notes:

- **Investments were made at a price approximately a month or later after each launch.**
- **Dividends received from Apple were reinvested into Apple stock the following year.**

Year [Model]	Phone Price	Launch	Total Invested Amount	Share Price	Shares Bought	Splits/Bonus	Dividend Per Share	Total Dividend	Total Shares So Far	Total Value
2007 [REAL]	$499	June/July	$499	$5.13	97	-	-	-	97	$499
2008 [3G]	$299	July/Aug	$299	$3.06	98	-	-	-	195	-
2009 [3GS]	$299	June/July	$299	$6.60	45	-	-	-	240	-
2010 [4]	$299	June/July	$299	$11.24	26	-	-	-	266	-
2011 [4S]	$399	Oct/Nov	$399	$14.06	28	-	-	-	295	-
2012 [5]	$649	Sep/Oct	$649	$18.55	34	-	$7.95 x 295	$2345	329	-
2013 [5S]	$649	Sep/Oct	$649+2345	$19.80	151	-	$11.80 x 329	$3882	480	-
2014 [6]	$649	Sep/Oct	$649+3882	$27.95	163	7:1	$6.81 x 480	$3268	3523	-
2015 [6S]	$649	Mar/Apr	$649+3268	$31.91	122	-	$2.03 x 3523	$7152	3645	-
2016 [SE]	$649	Sep/Oct	$649+7152	$28.99	269	-	$2.23 x 3645	$8128	3914	-
2017 [X]	$999	Sep/Nov	$999+8128	$42.31	216	-	$2.46 x 3914	$9628	4129	-
2018 [XS]	$999	Sep/Nov	$999+9628	$37.68	282	-	$2.82 x 4129	$11643	4411	-
2019 [11]	$699	Oct/Dec	$699+11643	$79.58	146	4:1	$3.08 x 4411	$13586	4557	-
2020 [12 Pro]	$1099	Sep/Nov	$1099+13586	$126.66	115	4:1	$2.015 x 18343	$36961	18343	-
2021 [13 Pro]	$1099	Sep/Nov	$1099+36961	$177.57	214	-	$0.88 x 18343	$16141	18557	-
2022 [14 Pro]	$1099	Dec/Feb	$1099+16141	$134.51	128	-	$0.91 x 18557	$16886	18685	-
2023 [15 Pro]	$1199	-	$1199+16886	$148.11	122	-	$0.95 x 18685	$17750	18807	-
2024 [15 Pro]	$1199	-	$1199+17750	$248	76	-	$1.00 x 18807	$18807	18883	? + 18807
Total	**$13,432**	-	**$179,842**	-	-	-	-	-	**18,883**	-

By January 2025, the person would have invested approximately **$13,432** in Apple stock since 2007. The total amount invested, including dividends, amounts to **$179,842**, and the total shares accumulated will be **18,883 shares**.

Note: The **$18,807** dividend received for 2024 is not included in the calculations, as the new model is yet to launch. Also, dividends have been added without considering tax implications to keep the calculation simple, as taxes depend on several factors.

What would $13,432 invested in Apple amount to? Take a guess!

Let's break it down and calculate -

As on 28 March 2025

"**As of March 2025,** Apple's stock price was **$221.53** per share.
Total investment value:
18,883 × 221.53 = **$4,183,150.99 + 18807 dividend [2024]**

"GUESS WHAT? YOU SAVED $13,432 ON PHONES AND TURNED IT INTO A JAW-DROPPING $4.36 MILLION IN JUST 18 YEARS—IMAGINE THE POTENTIAL STILL AHEAD!"

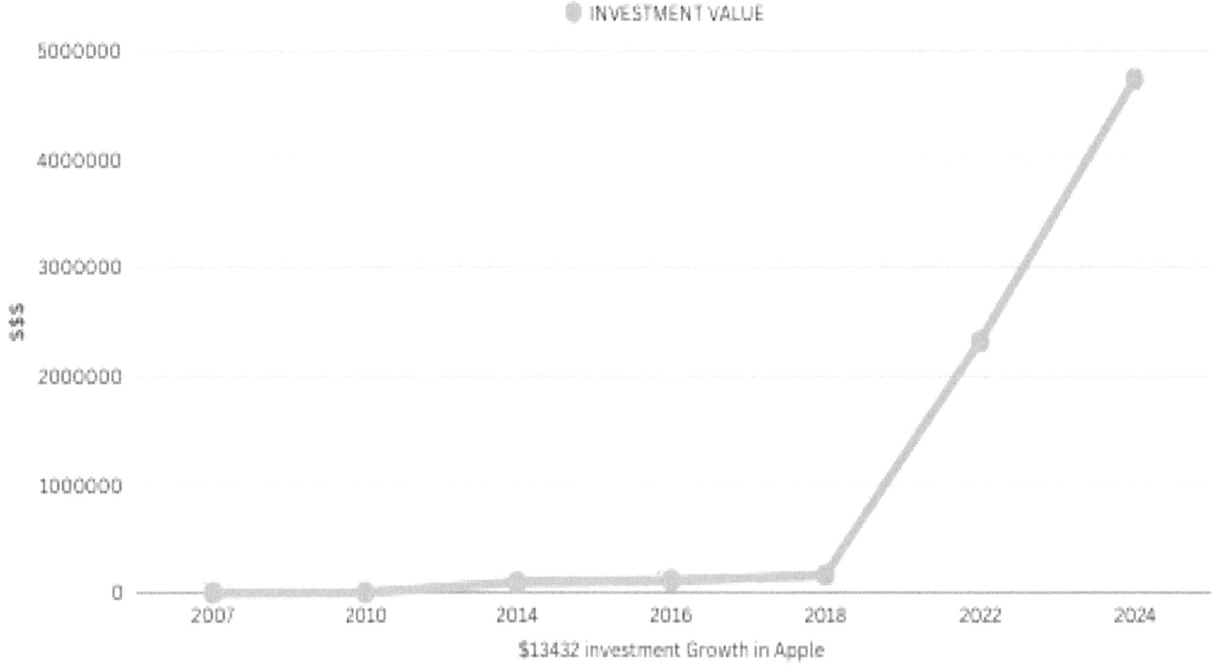

CONCLUSION -

This book has explored key financial principles, investment strategies, and economic trends, all aimed at helping you manage your finances wisely.

We've covered essential financial wisdom, drawing inspiration from classics like The Richest Man in Babylon, emphasizing minimizing expenses and building wealth. We've also delved into practical investment strategies, including homeownership, planning, and the power of disciplined saving and lending.

Beyond personal finance, we've examined broader economic insights, from global trends like the valuation of Russia's natural resources to the impact of AI on market leaders like Nvidia and Microsoft. We've also addressed the legal landscape of AI, including landmark copyright lawsuits.

Furthermore, we've provided practical advice on taxation and real estate, covering tax-deductible expenses like body corporate fees and home office costs, and explored the role of inflation and monetary policy in global financial stability.

"By applying these principles, you can confidently navigate your financial decisions and work toward maximizing long-term growth and stability."

"Thank you for taking the time to explore this book. I hope the insights and strategies shared within these pages empower you on your journey toward financial success. Your support means the world, and your feedback is deeply valued."

SUMMARY OF KEY THEMES

In this book, we explored essential financial principles, smart investment strategies, and the impact of economic trends and technological advancements on personal finance. By applying these insights, you can make informed decisions to secure your financial future.

Contact Information:

For more information, feedback, or inquiries, please contact:

Justwise Publications
P. O Box 1112

Mackay, QLD, 4740

AUSTRALIA.

Email Publishing@justwiseaccountingbooks.com

Author – Kirpal Singh

Thank you for reading!

Made in the USA
Middletown, DE
05 November 2026

36544999R10046